THE KENT
COLOURING BOOK

First published 2016
Reprinted 2018

The History Press
The Mill, Brimscombe Port
Stroud, Gloucestershire, GL5 2QG
www.thehistorypress.co.uk

British Library Cataloguing in Publication Data.
A catalogue record for this book is available from the British Library.

ISBN 978 0 7509 6805 8

Cover colouring by Lucy Hester.
Typesetting and origination by The History Press
Printed in Turkey

THE KENT
COLOURING BOOK

PAST AND PRESENT

Take some time out of your busy life to relax and unwind with this
feel-good colouring book designed for everyone who loves Kent.

Absorb yourself in the simple action of colouring in the scenes and settings from around the
county of Kent, past and present. From iconic architecture to picturesque coastal vistas, you are
sure to find some of your favourite locations waiting to be transformed with a splash of colour.
Bring these scenes alive as you de-stress with this inspiring and calming colouring book.

There are no rules – choose any page and any choice of colouring pens or pencils
you like to create your own unique, colourful and creative illustrations.

Dover Castle ▶

Fordwich ▶

Egerton Farmers' Market ▸

Dunorlan Park, Tunbridge Wells ▸

Kent & East Sussex Railway ▸

Ramsgate Royal Harbour ▸

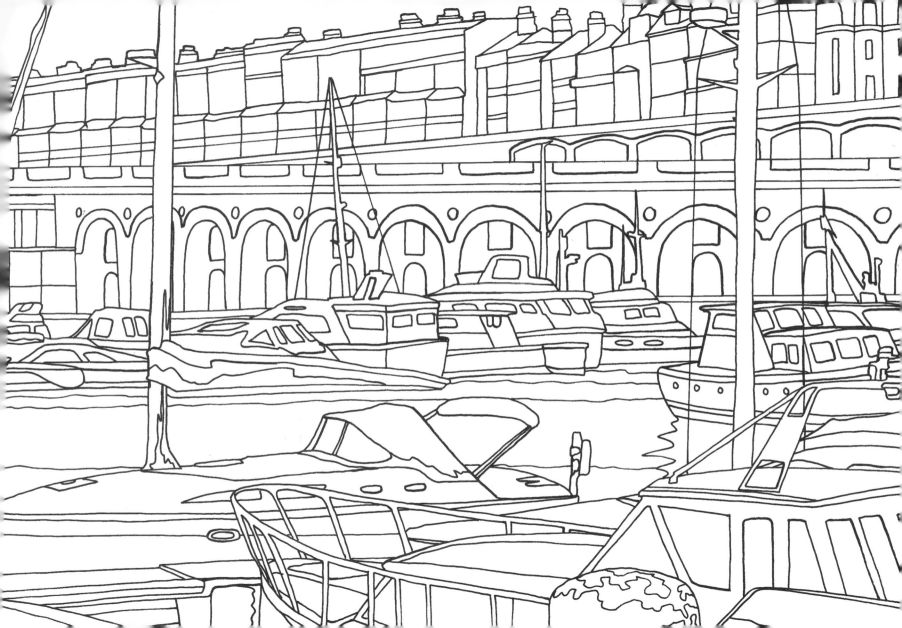

Theatre Royal interior, Margate ▸

Chatham Historic Dockyard ▶

Hever Castle ▶

Sandwich Quay ▸

Knole House, Sevenoaks ▶

Broadstairs, *c.* 1900 ▶

Mosaic at Lullingstone Roman Villa ▶

Tenterden ▶

Tonbridge Castle ▶

The now demolished Port Victoria station,
which once stood in the River Medway Estuary ▶

Tiger at Smarden Wildlife Heritage Foundation ▶

Whitstable Harbour ▶

Scotney Castle, Dover ▸

The Leas Lift, Folkestone ▶

Sissinghurst Castle Gardens ▶

Detail from the Shell Grotto, Margate ▸

The Pantiles, Royal Tunbridge Wells, *c.* 1895 ▸

Bluewater Shopping Mall, Greenhithe ▸

Godinton House, Ashford ▸

Port Lympne Reserve, Hythe ▸

Otford ▸

Canterbury Cathedral ▶

Giant Chess, Groombridge Place ▶

Aylesford ▶

Lavender at Downderry Nursery ▸

Ightham Mote, just outside Sevenoaks ▶

Faversham Creek ▶

Romney, Hythe & Dymchurch Railway ▸

Willesborough Windmill ▸

Deal Beach, 1904 ▸

Dreamland, Margate ▶

St Augustine's Abbey, Canterbury ▸

Rochester High Street ▶

Chilham Village ▸

Oast house, Brenchley ▶

The Sun Inn, Faversham ▸

Rochester Cathedral Tympanum ▶

Chartwell House, Westerham ▸

Leeds Castle, Maidstone ▸

Also from The History Press

THE LONDON
COLOURING BOOK
PAST AND PRESENT

Find this colouring book and more at
www.thehistorypress.co.uk

The
History
Press